DEDICATION

To my mom
the most inspiring woman in my life.

The love you have poured into the
generations of our family will leave a
kingdom legacy for generations to come.

Thank you for choosing me.

Inspiring Women—Who They Are and How To Be One

Second Edition, Revised
Copyright © 2021, 2017 by Sweet To The Soul Ministries
All rights reserved.
www.SweetToTheSoul.com

ISBN: 978-1-953718-05-1

Sweet To The Soul Press
PO Box 785
Royse City, Tx 75189

Original hand lettering by: Jana Kennedy-Spicer
Cover design and interior layout by: Jana Kennedy-Spicer

Unless noted otherwise, all scripture quotations are taken from the "ESV", The Holy Bible, English Standard Version Copyright © 2001 by Crossway, a publishing ministry of Good News Publishers. Used by permission. All rights reserved. ESV Text Edition: 2011

Scripture quotations marked "NIV" are taken from The Holy Bible: New International Version, NIV Copyright © 1973, 1978, 1984, 2011 by Biblicia, Inc. Used by permission. All rights reserved worldwide.

Scripture quotations marked MSG are taken from THE MESSAGE, copyright © 1993, 2002, 2018 by Eugene H. Peterson. Used by permission of NavPress, represented by Tyndale House Publishers. All rights reserved.

To order additional copies of this book and access additional resources, visit www.sweetothesoul.com/inspiring-women.htm

To inquire about ordering in quantities of 10 or more, please email info@sweettothesoul.com

A SOUL INSPIRED SCRIPTURE JOURNAL

INSPIRING WOMEN

WHO THEY ARE AND HOW TO BE ONE

Jana Kennedy- Spicer

Featuring: Stephanie K Adams

Carmen Horne - Mitzi Neely

Tyanne Rakowitz

SWEET TO THE SOUL PRESS

CONTENTS

the LORD
ANNOUNCES THE WORD
AND THE
WOMEN WHO
proclaim it
ARE A
MIGHTY
THRONG

PSALM 68:11 NIV

INTRODUCTION

We were running late and I was already impatient so when my daughter did not want to get in the car, but rather wanted to walk to school, my snippy response didn't really help the situation.

Walking to school meant a few minutes of freedom to my daughters. To me, it was half a mile out of my sight and an opportunity for anyone wanting to do them harm.

Over protective? Or justifiably cautious?

At their age, my brother and I walked to school with all the other kids on our block. We walked everywhere, all over our neighborhood, all day. As children, our parents also walked to school. Apparently it was miles from home, and up hill, both ways.

So when did walking to school become a bad thing? When bad people saw it as an opportunity to take advantage of children. Evil abounds.

No matter your age, I think we all would say the world that our kids and grand-kids are growing up in today is not the same world we grew up in. Some things are better for sure, but some things are far worse.

Our living family age span, as I write this, is 90 years. My mom, who lives with us now, celebrates her 92nd birthday soon, while our youngest grandchild is 2 years old.

While a lot has changed during those 90 years, many things have remained consistent. Like, our enemy the devil, has not slowed down causing division, suffering and strife. But, praise the Lord, *God is still God.*

> For if you remain silent at this time relief and deliverance for the Jews will arise from another place, but you and your father's family will perish. AND WHO KNOWS BUT THAT YOU HAVE COME TO YOUR ROYAL POSITION FOR SUCH A TIME AS THIS.
>
> Esther 4:14 NIV

There have been times in my life I would drift away day dreaming about living in the world my mom grew up in, slower paced days on a quiet country farm, no car, no tv, no social media; but then I remember how much I love indoor plumbing and Chick-Fil-A.

Truth is, THAT was her time; RIGHT NOW is my time. And for a long time, our times have overlapped. It was no accident when and where she was born, just as it was no accident when and where I was born or when and where you were born.

Know this friend, just as sure as Esther was born for her time and purpose, so were each and everyone of us.

THIS is our time. And these people in our lives, they are OUR people, to love, nurture, and inspire.

What a wonderful blessing it is for God to have created me a woman
and placed me in the family He chose for me. To have been raised,
prayed over and influenced by the inspiring women God surrounded me with.
To have been born to live on the patch of this Earth where God planted my feet.
To have been assigned to this specific time in history.
To have been entrusted with each beautiful soul in my family.

Who knows, but that I have come to this position for such a time as this. ✗

Who knows, but that you have come to your position for such a time as this.

So we're here. We have these people. How do we become the inspiring women God desires us to be?

Let's start by looking at what God's Word has to say about "inspire".

Inspiration ... We may not always be able to say when it will come, but I think we all know what inspiration does—*it moves us to action*. It is a catalyst. It lights a fire. It's an "ah-ha" moment. It's the light bulb over our head.

Inspiration motivates. It spurs us *to do*. ✗

Look at how "divine inspiration" is defined:

> *The infusion of ideas into the mind by the Holy Spirit; the conveying into the minds of men, ideas, notices or motions by extraordinary or supernatural influence; or the communication of the divine will to the understanding by suggestions or impres-*

sions on the mind, which leave no room to doubt the reality of their supernatural origin.

I love the word *infusion* used here....

- To penetrate
- To instill
- To inspire
- To steep or soak in
- To pour in

This is how the scriptures were written from the pens of many men, but the heart of The One God.

> *"All scripture is given by <u>inspiration</u> of God, and is profitable for doctrine,*
> *for reproof, for correction, for instruction in righteousness:"*
> 2 Timothy 3:16 KJV

The Greek word used here is *theopneustos*, which means *breathed out by God*. This verse is the only time this word occurs in the Bible.

Nothing else is divinely inspired like the Scriptures, they are as if God spoke them out directly to us.

> *"But there is a spirit in man: and the <u>inspiration</u> of the*
> *Almighty giveth them understanding."*
> Job 32:8 KJV

Here, Job uses the Hebrew word *neshamah* which means *the breath of God*. Interestingly, the same Hebrew word appears 23 times in Scripture and always refers to the life giving breath of God.

> *"And the LORD God formed man of the dust of the ground, and breathed*
> *into his nostrils the breath of life; and man became a living soul."*
> Genesis 2:7 KJV

Let's put these two together:

1. In Genesis, we see that God's breath brings life.

2. In Job, we learn that the spirit within us (the Holy Spirit) in combination with the inspiration of God (the life giving breath) gives us understanding and discernment.

So, what does this mean for us?

The breath of God which brought Adam to life is the same divine inspiration within us which brings the scriptures to life.

This type of inspiration is available to us today also. Not in the sense of the authors of the Bible, it is written, it is whole, it is complete. No the Holy Spirit will not inspire us to add to the writings of the Holy Bible.

But as believers and children of God, the Holy Spirit does pour in to us and inspire us to understanding and action.

> *"And the disciples were continually filled with joy and with the Holy Spirit."*
> Acts 13:52

We are told in Galatians 5 of the fruit of the Spirit, *the outward expression of the inward dwelling of the Holy Spirit.* Love, joy, peace, patience, kindness, goodness, faithfulness, gentleness and self-control are all the physical result of the Holy Spirt infusion into our lives.

If we stay in step with the Spirit, this infusion into our lives will inspire us into action!

> *"The fruit of the Spirit is love, joy, peace, patience, kindness, goodness, faithfulness, gentleness, self-control; ... If we live by the Spirit, let us also keep in step with the Spirit."*
> Galatians 2:22-23a, 25

When we do this, and live in accordance with God's teachings, it allows us to be women who inspire and influence generations for the kingdom. Our lives will begin to reflect what God has taught us from His Word and others will be able to see Him through us.

In truth, women carry great influence, especially over the next generation. Even while children are still in diapers or toddling around the house, women are raising little people who will one day become adults who will be influencers of the next generation. And know this, you do not have to be the parent to have influence in the life of someone. Some of my greatest influencers were not even family.

So we each need to ask ourselves, *"how will I influence those watching me?"* ✓

It is a personal decision each of us have to make. For sure, it requires us to be intentional in our efforts.

Are you ready to become the inspiring woman God has destined you to be?

Are you ready to accept His call to become the Kingdom influencer you were created to be?

This. Is. Our. Time.

WHO IN YOUR LIFE DO YOU WANT TO INFLUENCE FOR THE KINGDOM OF GOD?

Write their names below. Then take a moment to ask God to orchestrate divine opportunities for you to pour into their lives.

Meghan & Joey
Annie, Liam, Connor
Lydia
Ashley & Dan
my mom

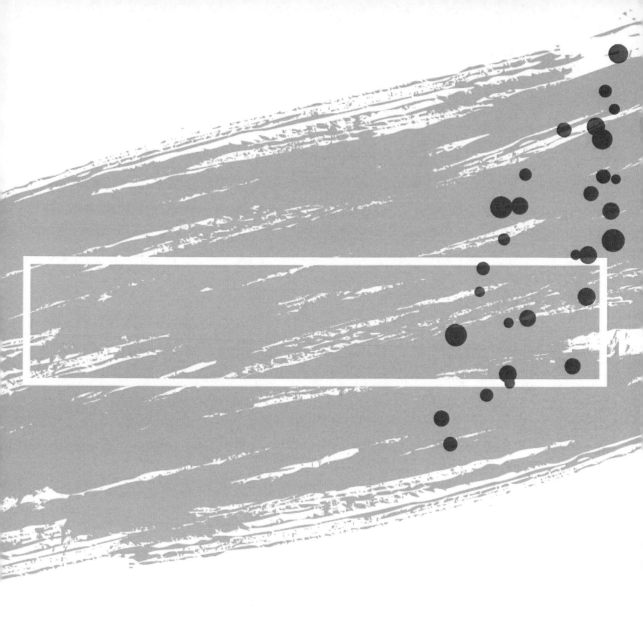

Thank you Lord for your life-giving breath in our lungs and for the divinely inspiring breath in our souls. As we study Your Word, we ask for the understanding that only you can give. We ask for your direction in how we should walk and what we should do so that we may be Kingdom influencers of generations to come.
In Jesus name, amen.

LEAVING A LEGACY

When I began my study of "*Inspiring Women*" the question which kept coming to mind was, "*what legacy of faith do I want to leave*?". Easily I could say that every Scripture on our reading list is a quality or characteristic which I aspire to emulate, as I am sure you would as well. But for time and page count, I decided to narrow the list to my top 5. The top 5 characteristics I want to focus on developing in my own life this year.

1. **Seek God First** - if I want to leave a legacy of faith, I must live a life of faith; and that propels me to seek after God.

2. **Speak with Wisdom** - in a time where there is no shortage of voices and opinions, I want the words I speak to be steeped in Godly wisdom.

3. **Be Strong** - spiritual warfare is in full force all around us, I want to be a woman of God who fights for her family.

4. **Express Gratitude** - we are living in a "me" world, recognizing and acknowledging blessings, helps me to shift the focus off of me and onto God.

5. **Give Testimony** - the world is full of people telling the next generation *not* to follow God, I want my kids and grand-children to not only know God that is real, but to know Him in a personal way.

Your top 5 Inspiring Women characteristics might be different. You may even think of one which is not on our list. So before we go any further, I urge you to take some time to look at our Scripture Reading List (pg. 21) in more detail and pray about the legacy of faith you desire to leave. Then select your top 5 and notate them on the following page.

Consider also why these 5 qualities have grabbed your heart. Is there someone special you want to inspire through a specific quality? Is there an area of your own life you sense God calling you to a season of growth? Maybe one of the Scriptures on our list touches on a specific area of spiritual warfare in your life.

Whatever the reason, notate it along with each of the 5 Inspiring Women characteristics you choose to record. (Don't skip this exercise, because we will refer back to it later.)

1

Notate, from the Scripture Reading List,
5 Inspiring Woman Characteristics you want
to devote to developing this coming year.
Include why this quality spoke to your heart .

2

THE LEGACY I WANT TO LEAVE

3

4

5

Character Traits of an Inspiring Woman

☐	Matthew 6:33-34	Seek God First
☐	Proverbs 31:26	Speak with Wisdom
☐	1 Timothy 2:9-10	Show True Beauty
☐	Philippians 2:3-5	Esteem Others
☐	Colossians 3:23	Work Diligently
☐	Joshua 1:9	Live with Courage
☐	1 Peter 3:4	Quiet their Spirit
☐	Psalm 1:2	Study God's Word
☐	1 Thessalonians 5:17	Pray Relentlessly
☐	2 Corinthians 9:11	Offer Generosity
☐	Psalm 38:18	Confess Faults
☐	Proverbs 17:22	Foster Joy
☐	Ecclesiastes 9:10	Complete Tasks Thoroughly
☐	Colossians 3:13	Forgive Others
☐	Romans 12:2	Stand Apart
☐	Psalm 100:4	Express Gratitude
☐	Ephesians 6:10	Stay Strong
☐	John 4:28-29	Give Testimony
☐	Proverbs 14:1	Build Up
☐	Ephesians 4:25	Talk Truthfully
☐	Philippians 2:2	Exercise Tolerance
☐	Titus 2:4-5	Shepherd Other Women
☐	1 Peter 1:22	Love Sincerely
☐	Proverbs 18:15	Pursue Knowledge
☐	Proverbs 19:2	Move with Caution
☐	1 John 3:17	Meet Needs of Others
☐	Romans 12:18	Live Peaceably
☐	Psalm 15:4	Keep their Word
☐	Galatians 1:10	Serve the Lord
☐	Galatians 6:9	Remain Steadfast
☐	Hebrews 13:2	Bestow Hospitality

Seek GOD FIRST

pray Relentlessly

live with courage

STUDY God's WORD

foster Joy

Confess FAULTS

FORgive others

WORK diligently

express Gratitude

SHOW TRUE beauty

Serve the Lord

Speak with wisdom

Talk Truthfully

esteem OTHERS

Build UP

offer generosity
stay Strong
LOVE sincerely
Keep THEIR WORD
Shepherd other women
give Testimony
quiet their Spirit
Live PEACEABLY
exercise tolerance
move with Caution
STAND apart
Meet other's Needs
pursue knowledge
Remain Steadfast
bestow hospitality

HER *delight* IS IN THE *law* OF THE LORD & ON HIS LAW SHE *meditates* DAY AND NIGHT

PSALM 1:2

LEARN ABOUT

INSPIRING WOMEN

In The Bible

CHARACTER STUDY METHOD

Have you ever wondered why the people mentioned in the Bible are mentioned in the Bible?

That may sound like an odd question, but I must admit that until a few years ago I had never asked that question.

One Sunday our pastor began a series on the genealogy of Jesus. A point of his teaching that stuck with me was that the names listed in the family tree of Jesus were all listed on purpose. The oddity of the time was that there were some women listed in this genealogy. Yet they were included on purpose. Knowing this leads us to ask, *why* were they included? *What* are we to learn from these women?

This lightbulb moment led me to begin looking at the people mentioned in the Bible in a whole new light—*especially the women.*

Why is this women mentioned in the Bible? *What* does God want me to learn from her? And *how* can I put into practice what I have learned from this woman.

Attempting to answer these questions, led me to a Bible study method of investigating specific people (women) in the Bible - Character Studies.

The foundational process of a Character Study uses the Inductive Bible Study method of observation, interpretation and application.

If you are not familiar with this Bible Study method, GotQuestions.org defines it like this: *"Inductive Bible study is an approach to God's Word focusing on three basic steps that move from a focus on specific details to a more general, universal principle. Through these three steps, we apply inductive reasoning, which is defined as the attempt to use information about a specific situation to draw a conclusion. The steps are observation (what does it say?), interpretation (what does it mean?), and application (what does it mean for my life?). Inductive Bible study is a valuable tool in understanding and applying the principles of God's Word. Inductive Bible study can be done on many different levels. The shorter version is good for a brief devotional. The more extensive study is wonderful for digging deeper into the mind and heart of God."*

As I sat down with my *"Inspiring Women"* Scripture Reading list, I prayed about the character traits God wanted me to focus on in my own life.

- Seek God First
- Speak with Wisdom
- Be Strong
- Express Gratitude
- Give Testimony

My starting point was set. These would be the first five character traits I would study.

The character studies which focus on Mary of Bethany (Seek God First), Abigail (Speak with Wisdom), and Deborah (Stay Strong) are all included in this Scripture journal.

Also included are blank Character Study pages for you to study other people of the Bible which exhibit the 5 character traits you selected from our Inspiring Women Scripture Reading List.

I learned so much from these women in the Bible. But God is impressing more on my heart. Just learning is not enough. Knowing the Scriptures is imperative for a child of God, but even the enemy knows the Scriptures.

At some point we must move beyond knowing.

AT SOME POINT IN OUR LIVES, KNOWING MUST BECOME DOING.

That's when true transformation occurs.

When the life we live everyday reflects the teachings of the Bible everyday, that's when we can inspire others— that is when generations are influenced for the kingdom.

So here is my challenge for you friend, for all of us really, to open these pages with the intent and expectation that when you close this Scripture Journal, you will be a different women. A woman that has been in the presence of God and it shows.

Let this journal serve as guide during your time in God's Word. When you read the words here, just imagine that you are not sitting alone, that I and others are there with you, and we are asking each other the questions in this journal. And we are answering them together, just as friends would discuss them if we were all gathered around the same table. Do not be intimidated by any question. Let the Holy Spirit guide your understanding.

Spend as much time as you need in the journal. Yes, there are 31 Scriptures and Character Traits included, but that doesn't mean you must rush through in just a month. Go at your own pace, but be intentional with your schedule. Set your time to spend with God and make that time a priority.

Then, after all that God teaches you through His Word, **be purposeful in letting it transform your life.** In the Application sections, be specific about what you *will do* with what you have learned. Identify actions which you can carry out but also ones which will grow your faith and character as a child of God.

Soul Friend, I am so looking forward to this journey with you. I have already learned so much, and I have definitely been challenged in applying what God has taught me.

This is our time right now, we are not alive at this time in history by accident, the people in our lives are not there by accident. God is calling us to be women who inspire generations for the Kingdom.

Will you join me in accepting this call?

NAME: Name of the person being studied.

SCRIPTURE: Passage of Scripture being studied.

Write out the Scripture passage being referenced for this character study. Reach beyond a single Bible verse to include the context of the passage. List other Scriptures which also relate to the main passage or where the person being studied is mentioned again.

CHARACTER TRAIT: Main character trait of the person being studied.

List the main character trait or traits this person exhibits within the Scripture passage studied.

OBSERVATION: What does the Scripture passage say?

1. Pray for the Holy Spirit's guidance. Read and reread the passage. Read it in another version of the Bible if available.

2. Gather all sorts of facts like an investigative reporter. Ask questions to help you observe the facts: Who? What happened? What was taught? When? Where? How? Why? This is where you see and discover what the author is saying.

3. Use Bible study helps like commentaries to get a clearer meaning. On-line sites like BibleHub.com and BibleStudyTools.com provide great resources with multiple translations of the Bible as well as many commentary and sermon resources.

4. Examples of observation questions to ask:

   - What are the basic facts of the passage?

   - What does this passage of Scripture reveal to me about God?

   - Who is mentioned in this passage and what are some things from the text we learn about them?

   - What is the theme or main point of the passage?

INTERPRETATION: What does this Scripture passage mean?

1. What is the author's intent in this passage? What is the one principle or lesson the writer / God was trying to communicate?

2. Look at other scriptures which relate to the passage. What do other verses say about this thought or idea?

3. Are there any words or phrases which need definition? Use a Bible Dictionary to look them up and understand the passage better.

4. Examples of interpretation questions to ask:

    • How might you summarize what the passage teaches?

    • What is the main point of the passage?

    • What is the author trying to get across in this passage?

    • Why do you think God put this passage in the Bible?

APPLICATION: How does this principle apply to one specific area of my life?

1. What is the Holy Spirit saying to you in this passage? Ask Him.

2. How does the Scripture passage relate to the here and now?

3. Consider how you can apply the heart of the massage to your life. Identify what will you do differently because of what you learned.

4. Examples of application questions to ask:

    • How might we build into our lives the truths of this passage? When / where might we apply them?

    • What behavior does this passage call for?

    • How might you put into practice what you have learned?

    • Write out various ways you can build this character trait into your life.

MAKE A PLAN: Put what you learned into practice.

1.   How can we put into practice what we are learning from this passage?

2.   Make a plan specific to you: Identify 3 specific actions to take.

3.   How can you use what you have learned from (person studied) to build a legacy within your family?

Consider how you can use what you have learned to influence those around you.
Ask God to help you identify someone specific and identify how you can intentionally apply the lesson learned from this passage as you interact with this person.

NOTES: Use this space for any additional notes on the person or passage studied.

PRAYER: Write out your personal prayer to God.

YOU ARE ANXIOUS & TROUBLED ABOUT MANY THINGS BUT ONE THING IS NECESSARY

LUKE 10:41-42 ESV

MARY OF BETHANY

SCRIPTURE: Luke 10:38-42 ESV

38 Now as they went on their way, Jesus entered a village. And a woman named Martha welcomed him into her house. 39 And she had a sister called Mary, who sat at the Lord's feet and listened to his teaching. 40 But Martha was distracted with much serving. And she went up to him and said, "Lord, do you not care that my sister has left me to serve alone? Tell her then to help me." 41 But the Lord answered her, "Martha, Martha, you are anxious and troubled about many things, 42 but one thing is necessary. Mary has chosen the good portion, which will not be taken away from her."

CHARACTER TRAIT:

Seeking God First

OBSERVATION:

1. Who is she? Where did she live? Who is her family?

Mary is a friend and follower of Jesus. She lived in Bethany, a village near Jerusalem. She has a sister named Martha and a brother named Lazarus.

2. In what circumstances does Mary find herself?

Mary and her sister Martha have welcomed Jesus into their home. Verse 38 mentions "they", meaning that Jesus was not alone. He was traveling with his disciples and most likely a crowd was following. So even though verse 38 says "..*Martha welcomed HIM into her house..*" (emphasis mine) probably over a dozen men were with Jesus. Martha was attending to all of the guests, as a good hostess does. However, she was doing this all on her own, as her sister Mary was sitting at the feet of Jesus with her attention focused on him alone.

INTERPRETATION:

1. **What are some ideas as to the most important things this passage communicates?**

Well, first, it is NOT telling us that being attentive to our guests is bad, in fact, the Bible commends entertaining others in several places.

However, given that Jesus himself was one of the these guests, the opportunity to sit with him and listen to him teach had to be rare. Given the choice to serve her guests—which was a good thing to do—or spend time with Jesus, Mary chose to do what Jesus himself referred to as the "good portion", sit at the feet of Jesus.

2. **What character traits did Mary display in this passage?**

Mary purposefully sought out to spend time with Jesus instead of letting the circumstances in which she found herself, distract her.

> NEVER BE SO BUSY SERVING FOR GOD TO NEGLECT SPENDING TIME WITH GOD

APPLICATION:

1. **What lesson can we learn from Mary?**

If I wait until I have "free time" after all of my responsibilities have been taken care of, to spend time with God, I am not choosing "the good portion".

2. **In what ways does this passage and lesson challenge our modern day values and lifestyle?**

Culture tells us to do more, work harder, be better, achieve more. i.e.: Our neighbor hosted 12 for fellowship, so I must entertain 20. My co-workers work xx hours a week, so I must work more to get ahead. We see this even in our churches. The church down the street has a larger attendance, so our church must increase the entertainment to draw people.

Opening our homes to others is actually a good Biblical thing. Working diligently is also a good thing, and Biblical. Growing the church body is wonderful and yes, Biblical. However, all of these things become the "lesser portion" when we focus on them instead of first seeking and spending time with God.

MAKE A PLAN:

1. How can we put into practice what we are learning from this passage?

SCHEDULE IT. BE INTENTIONAL IN PRIORITIZING TIME WITH GOD. Put it on the calendar. Instead of waiting until "I have time", I will make time.

USE A MAP. FOLLOW A DAILY SCRIPTURE READING PLAN OR LIST. Having a reading plan to follow gives me a great starting point.

WRITE IT DOWN. KEEP A JOURNAL OF MY CONVERSATIONS WITH GOD. Writing down what I learn, what I am praying for, and what God is telling me, not only helps me remember but gives me something to go back and revisit to see how God is walking with me.

2. Make a plan specific to you:

SCHEDULE IT.

USE A MAP.

WRITE IT DOWN.

3. How can you use what you have learned from Mary of Bethany to build a legacy within your family?

NOTES:

_____

_____

_____

_____

_____

_____

_____

_____

_____

_____

_____

_____

_____

PRAYER: (write out your personal prayer below)

Father God, thank you for the privilege of spending time with You. Forgive me for taking this for granted and putting other things before You. Give me the desire to spend more time with You and the strength to always choose the good portion. In Jesus' name, Amen.

Tips for Developing a Habit of Quiet Time

1. PICK A PLACE

Decide where you will be everyday for your quiet time. Select a location free from distractions where you can focus. Be sure to stock any needed supplies like your Bible, journal, pens, pencils and highlighters. A Bible study or reference materials might also be helpful. And I always have my fav beverage with me too.

2. SCHEDULE A TIME

Set aside a specific amount of time every-day and add it to your calendar / planner. Start with just 10 to 15 minutes. Consistency is the key here, and as you develop a daily habit of quiet time, the amount of time you spend with God will naturally increase.

Choose a time which works for you. I tried for years to have a "morning quiet time" but mornings in our house were anything but quiet. Then I heard someone say they had their quiet time at night. That was perfect for my natural rhythm and season of life.

3. DETERMINE THE FORMAT

Determine the structure to your quiet time. How will you spend your time with God? Base this on your desired goals. If you want to increase your Biblical knowledge, incorporate a Bible Study or sermon resources. Or plan to spend more time in prayer if you want to develop more intimacy with God. You may want to mix up this format every few weeks to keep your quiet time fresh and engaging.

4. JUST DO IT!

Even with all the planning and scheduling, developing a consistent quiet time routine comes down to actually doing it. Discipline requires consistency. So make the decision to follow through and spend time with God every day. But allow yourself some grace. If something conflicts with your scheduled time, make it up later in the day. If you have less available time one day, listen to a devo or Bible teaching via podcast. Consistent yet flexible. God is available whenever and wherever you call on Him.

SHE OPENS HER
MOUTH WITH WISDOM
& THE TEACHING OF
KINDNESS
IS ON HER TONGUE.

PROVERBS 31:26 ESV

NAME:

ABIGAIL

SCRIPTURE: 1 Samuel 25:1-43 ESV (verses 3, 14, 17-19, 23, 28, 32-22 shown)

3 Now the name of the man was Nabal, and the name of his wife Abigail. The woman was discerning and beautiful, but the man was harsh and badly behaved; he was a Calebite. 14 But one of the young men told Abigail, Nabal's wife, "Behold, David sent messengers out of the wilderness to greet our master, and he railed at them. 17 Now therefore know this and consider what you should do, for harm is determined against our master and against all his house, and he is such a worthless man that one cannot speak to him." 18 Then Abigail made haste and took two hundred loaves and two skins of wine and five sheep already prepared and five seahsa of parched grain and a hundred clusters of raisins and two hundred cakes of figs, and laid them on donkeys. 19 And she said to her young men, "Go on before me; behold, I come after you." But she did not tell her husband Nabal. 23When Abigail saw David, she hurried and got down from the donkey and fell before David on her face and bowed to the ground. 28 Please forgive the trespass of your servant. For the LORD will certainly make my lord a sure house, because my lord is fighting the battles of the LORD, and evil shall not be found in you so long as you live. 32And David said to Abigail, "Blessed be the LORD, the God of Israel, who sent you this day to meet me! 33Blessed be your discretion, and blessed be you, who have kept me this day from bloodguilt and from working salvation with my own hand!

CHARACTER TRAIT:

Speak with Wisdom

OBSERVATION:

1.   Who is she? Where did she live? Who is her family?

Abigail is the wife to a wealthy land owner named Nabal, who is foolish and ungenerous. His name literally means "fool".

2.   In what circumstances does Abigail find herself?

Abigail has just learned that (next in line to be king) David made a request to her husband Nabal for provisions for he and some of his men. But Nabal's interaction with David's messenger was rude and offensive. Nabal dismissed the messenger, disrespected David and refused to provide any food or assistance. David in response was greatly offended and gathered 400 of his men, armed with swords, and set off to settle the offense intent on killing Nabal .

So Abigail quickly and quietly jumps into action, preparing the requested supplies and sending her servants out to intercept David. When Abigail arrives, she humbles herself before David, takes responsibility for her husband's bad temperament and poor manners then begs David's forgiveness. David's anger is calmed by her manner and concedes, receiving the provisions and withdraws from killing Nabal.

INTERPRETATION:

1. What are some ideas as to the most important things this passage communicates?

This situation with Nabal and Abigail gives us a relatable example of the foolish vs. the wide. Abigail's actions were very bold in that she devised a solution and executed it without the knowledge or consent of her husband; whose earlier response to David had marked them for certain death. Abigail's intervention with David perfectly illustrates Proverbs 15:1, "A soft answer turns away wrath, but a harsh word stirs up anger."

2. What character traits did Abigail display in this passage?

Abigail was able to very quickly discern the consequences of the hasty actions by Nabal. But even more, she displayed astute wisdom when she was able to assess what needed to be done to rectify the offense and respond with urgency and humility.

She even took on the responsibility of her husbands actions when confronting David instead of blaming the rightful offender, Nabal.

> DON'T LET MY PRIDE GET IN THE WAY OF GOD'S PROMPTING.

APPLICATION:

1. What lesson can we learn from Abigail?

Abigail displayed not only discernment and wisdom but a willingness to respond and take action. It is one thing to KNOW what needs to be done, and quite another to actually DO it.

2. How might we build into our lives the truths of this passage? When / where might we apply them?

- To set our pride aside so we can rightly see the need of others.

- To filter our responses through the Holy Spirit so we can rightly discern everything about the situation.

- To be willing to act on the prompting of the Holy Spirit = exercising the wisdom given.

The lesson learned from Abigail's actions can definitely be utilized on a daily basis. We may not have an army of 400 at our door, but we are open to conflict through our everyday life. Offenses can be easily found whether they are intended or not. We may not be able to control another person's words or responses, but with the help of the Holy Spirit, we can control our own.

MAKE A PLAN:

1. How can we put into practice what we are learning from this passage?

LISTEN. LISTEN WITH AN OPEN HEART to what others are saying with the intention of understanding instead of responding. Consider also what is not being said; and clarify what is really meant by what is said.

PAUSE. PAUSE AND PRAY, ASKING GOD FOR DISCERNMENT, wisdom and direction. Then wait for his response. If needed, step away from the situation to gain perspective.

RESPOND. RESPOND WITH GRACE AND HUMILITY. Don't offer an emotion fueled response. Be ready to take whatever action God directs.

2. Make a plan specific to you:

LISTEN.

PAUSE.

RESPOND.

3. How can you use what you have learned from Abigail to build a legacy within your family?

NOTES:

PRAYER: (write out your personal prayer below)

Father God, thank You for entrusting me with the people in my life. Help me to filter my words through You and to speak not only with wisdom but with kindness. Lead me to use my words to connect with others in a manner which glorifies You. In Jesus' name, Amen.

Scriptures to Pray for Wisdom

"...that their hearts may be encouraged, being knit together in love, to reach all the riches of full assurance of understanding and the knowledge of God's mystery, which is Christ, in whom are hidden all the treasures of wisdom and knowledge. I say this in order that no one may delude you with plausible arguments." Colossians 2:2-4

"If any of you lacks wisdom, let him ask God, who gives generously to all without reproach, and it will be given him. But let him ask in faith, with no doubting, for the one who doubts is like a wave of the sea that is driven and tossed by the wind. For that person must not suppose that he will receive anything from the Lord; he is a double-minded man, unstable in all his ways." James 1:5-8

"The fear of the Lord is the beginning of wisdom, and knowledge of the Holy One is understanding. For through wisdom your days will be many, and years will be added to your life. If you are wise, your wisdom will reward you; if you are a mocker, you alone will suffer." Proverbs 9:10-12 NIV

"...That the God of our Lord Jesus Christ, the Father of glory, may give you the Spirit of wisdom and of revelation in the knowledge of him, having the eyes of your hearts enlightened, that you may know what is the hope to which he has called you, what are the riches of his glorious inheritance in the saints..." Ephesians 1:17-18

"Blessed is the one who finds wisdom, and the one who gets understanding, for the gain from her is better than gain from silver and her profit better than gold. She is more precious than jewels, and nothing you desire can compare with her. Long life is in her right hand; in her left hand are riches and honor. Her ways are ways of pleasant-ness, and all her paths are peace. She is a tree of life to those who lay hold of her; those who hold her fast are called blessed." Proverbs 3:13-18

FINALLY,
BE STRONG
IN THE LORD &
IN THE STRENGTH
OF HIS MIGHT.

EPHESIANS 6:10 ESV

NAME:

DEBORAH

SCRIPTURE: Judges ch 4 & 5; 4:4-10 ESV featured

4 Now Deborah, a prophetess, the wife of Lappidoth, was judging Israel at that time. 5 She used to sit under the palm of Deborah between Ramah and Bethel in the hill country of Ephraim, and the people of Israel came up to her for judgment. 6 She sent and summoned Barak the son of Abinoam from Kedesh-naphtali and said to him, "Has not the LORD, the God of Israel, commanded you, 'Go, gather your men at Mount Tabor, taking 10,000 from the people of Naphtali and the people of Zebulun. 7 And I will draw out Sisera, the general of Jabin's army, to meet you by the river Kishon with his chariots and his troops, and I will give him into your hand'?" 8 Barak said to her, "If you will go with me, I will go, but if you will not go with me, I will not go." 9 And she said, "I will surely go with you. Nevertheless, the road on which you are going will not lead to your glory, for the LORD will sell Sisera into the hand of a woman." Then Deborah arose and went with Barak to Kedesh. 10 And Barak called out Zebulun and Naphtali to Kedesh. And 10,000 men went up at his heels, and Deborah went up with him.

CHARACTER TRAIT:

Stay Strong

OBSERVATION:

1. Who is she? Where did she live? Who is her family?

Deborah was a prophetess, a wife, a judge of Israel, she was sought out by the people for judicial decisions, she was a warrior and instructed the General in battle.

2. What are some things in the text that we learn about her?

As a prophetess, she had the ability to discern the mind and purpose of God and to declare this to others. She was divinely inspired. She was one of five female Old Testament prophets. [1]

As a judge, she was a leader of Israel raised up by God to deliver His people from the bondage their idolatry had caused. All of Israel was under her jurisdiction and after the conquest of the Canaanites, she ruled in peace for 40 years. [1]

As a warrior, she led Israel's army of 10,000 to victory against Sisera's 100,000 fighters. [1]

1 "All The Women of The Bible" by Herbert Lockyer, Zondervan 1967

INTERPRETATION:

1. **What is the author's intent in this passage? What is the one principle or lesson the writer / God was trying to communicate?**

In Deborah we see a strong leader and warrior. Her strength comes from her faith in and relationship with God. Just as with other OT prophets (male), she has an unwavering belief that what God has spoken to her will come to pass. This gives her the strength to step forward into situations against great odds with complete confidence in God.

2. **Why do you think God put this passage in the Bible?**

Historically, for the Israelites to remember generation after generation how God would do what He promises, and deliver them from captivity.

On a personal level, we are similar to Deborah in that God is also our source of strength. He uses the faithful to accomplish great things in a manner which leaves no doubt it was only by God's hand, not mans.

> **GOD MAY SEND ME INTO BATTLE, BUT ONLY HE CAN DELIVER THE VICTORY.**

APPLICATION:

1. **What lesson can we learn from Deborah?**

I am just a weapon in the hands of God. He may send me into battles, large and small, but only He can deliver the victory.

God is faithful to His Word even today. What He says He will do, He will do. That truth is our source of confidence. Not in ourselves, but in Him.

2. **How does this passage challenge or encourage in this particular life season?**

It seems spiritual warfare is around every corner and most of the time I feel outnumbered. But maybe that is the perfect setting for God to show up.

I am challenged because I feel God calling me off of the bench and into the "game". This battle may look different for me than it does you and often it seems like the enemy is winning.

But I am also encouraged because Deborah has shown me that it is God's battle to win and He will give me the strength for the fight.

MAKE A PLAN:

1. How can we put into practice what we are learning from this passage?

BE AWARE OF THE ENEMY. THE ENEMY AND HIS MINIONS ARE SNEAKY and they prowl around in the shadows and move under the disguise of false truths. To recognize their deceit and lies, I must know God's truth.

PLACE MY CONFIDENCE IN GOD. I DO NOT HAVE THE STRENGTH FOR THE FIGHT ON MY OWN. Victory is only possible if I stay in God's will and in right relationship with Him.

SHOW UP FOR BATTLE. WHEN GOD CALLS ME, I MOST GO WITHOUT HESITATION . Genuine faith in God and His Word and His plans will propel me to go when and where God directs. Doubt will keep me scared and tangled up in the weeds.

2. Make a plan specific to you:

BE AWARE OF THE ENEMY.

PLACE MY CONFIDENCE IN GOD.

SHOW UP FOR BATTLE.

3. How can you use what you have learned from Deborah to build a legacy within your family?

NOTES:

PRAYER: (write out your personal prayer below)

Father God, thank You for your strength and guidance. My heart so desires to be a kingdom warrior. To be strong and wise like Deborah. I know in my own strength I fail, but with Your strength all things are possible. Help me to step out in faith when you call me to action. In Jesus' name, Amen.

Scriptures to Help You Stay Strong

Fear not, for I am with you; be not dismayed, for I am your God; I will strengthen you, I will help you, I will uphold you with my righteous right hand.
Isaiah 41:10

The **LORD** is my strength and my song, and he has become my salvation; this is my God, and I will praise him, my father's God, and I will exalt him.
Exodus 15:2

My flesh and my heart may fail, but **God** is the strength of my heart and my portion forever
Psalm 73:26.

But the Lord is faithful. He will establish you and guard you against the evil one.
2 Thessalonians 3:3

Be on your guard; stand firm in the faith; be courageous; be strong.
1 Corinthians 16:13 NIV

Take time to commit each Scripture to memory and be prepared when the enemy tries to trip you up with doubt.

NOTEWORTHY

Teach WHAT IS GOOD & SO TRAIN THE *young women* TO LOVE THEIR HUSBAND AND CHILDREN

TITUS 2:4

MEET THESE
INSPIRING WOMEN
In Our Lives

THE LOVE OF A MOTHER

MITZI NEELY

I've always wondered how I could be so blessed to have not one, but two women in my life who nurtured me, encouraged me, and inspired me to be all I can be. Each of them represents differences, but they also share similarities. One I've had for 58 years. The other for 35 years. My mom, Amelia Rowland, and my mother-in-law, Lalon Neely Pirkey, are the best of both worlds.

Both women endured challenges and hardships in their lives.

One was born during the Great Depression. The other experienced the Great Depression. Each lost an adult child, suffered the loss of a spouse, and were blessed to remarry and enjoy happy lives.

One was an educator. The other, a businesswoman. And they shared similar skill sets that include detailed, organized, well-informed, astute, and savvy. They enjoyed their careers and performed to the highest level.

I have learned so much from them over the years. They taught me that loving God was first, and that family was the heartbeat of your existence. While each differed in their talents and abilities, they both loved people, and treasured their children and grandchildren.

They each possessed the kind of strength, character, integrity, and morals that were non-negotiables. Each of them showed me it would be difficult to survive the daily doses of life without the Fruit of the Spirit. Their shining examples are forever etched in my soul.

"BUT THE FRUIT OF THE SPIRIT IS LOVE, JOY, PEACE, FORBEARANCE, KINDNESS, GOODNESS, FAITHFULNESS, GENTLENESS AND SELF-CONTROL. AGAINST SUCH THINGS THERE IS NO LAW."
GALATIANS 5:22-23

My two mothers were poster girls for confidence, and their courage and perseverance carried them through the tough times. They encountered setbacks, endured tragedies, and picked themselves up more times then they cared to count, but it's who they were. Their kindness and graciousness extended beyond their families to friends and acquaintances alike. In the years since becoming a wife and mother, I have witnessed countless times how important it is to be gracious, kind, thoughtful, forgiving, courageous, and respectful of others. I try to model those same attributes daily.

"SHE OPENS HER MOUTH WITH WISDOM, AND THE TEACHING OF KINDNESS IS ON HER TONGUE."
PROVERBS 31:26

Their teachings equipped me with confidence, passion, godly thinking, and spiritual awareness, so I can face the circumstances and challenges of this life.

As I reflect on, and treasure what I've learned from these two beautiful women over the years, it comes down to a simple, but powerful list.

- Seek God First
- Encourage and love one another
- Never lower your standards or expectations
- Be a role model, for you never know who is watching, and
- Share a mixture of grace, love, and laughter everywhere you go.

I am who I am today because of my two mothers. They loved me, instructed me, counseled me, advised me, and modeled for me. I am forever grateful for their selflessness, their joy filled hearts, and for wanting me to be all that God intended.

A LEGACY OF HEAVEN

STEPHANIE K. ADAMS

For as long as I can remember, she was waiting for Heaven. I often wonder if she ever really accepted this world as her home. She certainly fully embraced life here with her family. She was a daughter, sister, wife, mother, and she was my grandmother.

We called her Mamaw. She was kind and loving, but she expected us to act respectfully and be obedient. If she or Papaw said to do something, we knew we had only one chance to get it done; there would be no other opportunity before they handed out discipline.

We spent summers helping tend to the garden, canning vegetables, and hanging laundry on clotheslines. We would have cookouts at the lake and spend days fishing and swimming.

Mamaw taught us the Ten Commandments and Psalm 23 by giving us a dime for every commandment or verse we could memorize and one whole dollar if we could recite each completely. She kept an old hymnal from the church in the bookcase and would teach me to sing.

Every night before bed, she and Papaw would recite the Lord's prayer as they whispered it together in unison. Then my favorite memory of them was three small kisses—smack, smack, smack.

She loved Jesus more than anyone I've ever known. Talk about God, Heaven, and the Bible was normal, everyday conversation that started as far back as my memories.

At first, she would read a few verses aloud as I sat on her lap, then as I grew and had to move to the sofa, she began to explain to me what we had read.

Even from an early age, she spoke matter-of-factly about Heaven and how she would go there one day. As time marched on, so did our conversations about Heaven, death, and what it would be like while she waited for me to arrive on the other side of this earth.

Our talks were deep yet straightforward. Mamaw never shied away from telling me how much she loved me but always making sure I was prepared for when she would leave this life for the one with Jesus.

Her way of speaking about Heaven was never scary for me, even as a young child. Mamaw filled her words with joy, hope, and truth. It was apparent this place she told me about not only exists, but her love for it was tangible, noticeably different than when other folks discussed Heaven. Like it was a place to be aware of but not to be spoken about because doing so would acknowledge the uncomfortable, not-to-be-discussed topic of dying.

"FOR THIS WORLD IS NOT OUR PERMANENT HOME; WE ARE LOOKING FORWARD TO A HOME YET TO COME."

HEBREWS 13:14 NLT

As Mamaw grew older, I would often visit with her once a week as my refuge from the hard of life. We spent time watching her favorite talk show in silence, then discussing the craziness of it all during commercials. Afterward, she would turn the TV off, go into the kitchen, and dip us both a cup of ice cream. We would listen to whatever was troubling each other, and then she would pick up her Bible and read a few verses.

She would allow a long pause filled with silence as if she was giving space for the weight of God's wisdom to settle in our spirits, and then she would ask, "What do you think that means?".

Without fail, we would conclude each visit with talk of the day she would leave and how she anticipated I would feel. She would encourage me not to become too sad or lonely with her absence.

While Mamaw loved her life here, she lived Heaven-bound, never fully embracing earth as her final destination, always waiting for her return trip Home. She was prepared and ready for when it was finally her time to leave. She made sure she left a legacy of Heaven behind for those she loved.

In fact, at her funeral, the pastor handed each of us individual pamphlets that Mamaw had chosen for us. There staring back at me was her handwriting highlighting text and encouraging me it was okay to cry but not to let grief linger. She made sure she was there to comfort me, even from the other side of Heaven.

The last meaningful conversation I had with Mamaw, we sat in rocking chairs on the front porch of the facility that had become her home. It was a beautiful spring day with a bright blue cloudless sky, and we held hands as we rocked in silence, just enjoying each other's company.

She broke the silence as she looked up at the sky, *"I sure am ready to go whenever God wants me."*

"I sure will miss you, Mamaw."

"I know. I'll miss you, too."

"What do you think you'll say when you finally get there?"

"Thank you, Jesus! It's about time!"

We laughed as she squeezed my hand.

A few months later, at the age of 99, she finally left for Home. I have no doubt when she arrived she threw open her arms and proclaimed with a big smile, "It's about time!"

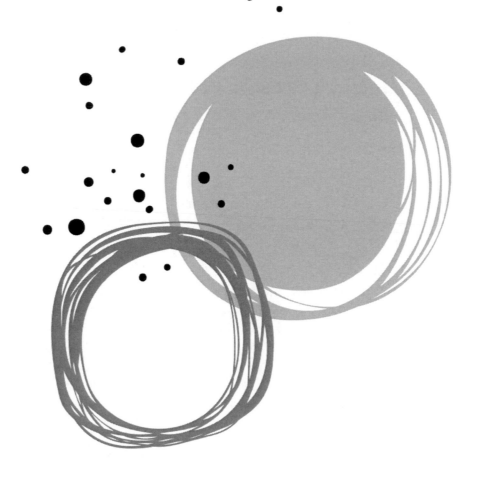

Thank you Lord for godly women who make the difference
in the lives of children. Help us to remember Your love for
little ones when our time seems as short as our patience.
Open our eyes to those around us that need our
love and influence.
In the name of Jesus, amen.

Carmen Horne

STATION WAGONS & ICE CREAM

CARMEN HORNE

Her station wagon was filled with children and camping gear. Not tents and sleeping bags, but the stuff we would need to live a week at church camp.

Our laughs and giggles hung in the air as we loaded. For those of us who had attended summer church camp in past years, we knew what fun lay ahead.

What makes a school teacher want to spend summers hauling children to camp? Sister Mara Larche was one of those teachers.

Travel time to Camp Pollock was 2+ hours. Midway was our ice cream stop. Long before Burger Barn made Olla, Louisiana famous - and became the must stop for campers - Girod's was there. Sis. Larche always stopped to buy us an ice cream cone. Does ice cream ever taste better than summertime, no air conditioning, and friends headed to camp together?

It was at church camp that I first gave my life to Jesus Christ. I had been to church since birth, but I actually began a personal relationship with Him at Camp Pollock.

Camp changed my life. I could write forever on my fond memories. That was back in the day when we slept in open-air cabins (we sweltered at bedtime and were shivering by daylight), showered in bath houses that usually had a frog or two in the shower stall with you, attended service in an open-air sanctuary, and swam with only girls – no boys allowed.

Did Sis. Larche realize her impact? Did she know that one day I would honor her for her commitment to get a bunch of kids to camp? Oh, did she realize my special memories of camp would plant a seed that would make me ensure my daughter and her friends attended summer camp at Camp Pollock?

Impacting lives happens when we are willing to give without the promise of getting.

Sis. Larche never married and had no biological children, but she had a quiver full of spiritual kids. Her investment into us has made a difference generation after generation.

A hostess for countless wedding and baby showers at church (including mine), a Sunday School teacher, and helping out in Bible School is how I remember her. I once heard that she bought a sewing machine for a woman in our community because she needed it to earn an income and hers had stopped working. Sis. Larche devoted her life to people, ministry.

She was honored as Louisiana Teacher of the Year and was an ordained minister and pastored several churches.

Enjoy these dear memories of Sis. Mara Larche:

> She headed up making a quilt for me and Jack. I still have it and use it regularly. I remember her with fondness and love. She was a woman of God.   Linda L.

> Her example, her prayers, her faithfulness, her sweet smile. She was an example for all Christians to go by. Dianne Y.

> She lived to serve the Lord by loving and serving others. She loved to teach and preach. She loved the long hours of preparation, reading, and studying her Bible and books.   Sarah K.

> She was a great teacher for church and school. If a child didn't get a gift off the Christmas tree at church, she always had one to give them. Marie W.

Mara Larche taught by example. Oh, she taught with books, and papers, and pencils, and chalkboards, but mostly by her life well lived.

"DO NOTHING FROM SELFISH AMBITION OR CONCEIT, BUT IN HUMILITY COUNT OTHERS MORE SIGNIFICANT THAN YOURSELVES. LET EACH OF YOU LOOK NOT ONLY TO HIS OWN INTERESTS, BUT ALSO TO THE INTERESTS OF OTHERS."

PHILIPPIANS 2:3-4 ESV

ONE FAMILY. ONE CHILD. A FRIENDSHIP. A GIFT.

TYANNE RAKOWITZ

Have you ever heard, "blood is thicker than water?" When you hear this, what's your first thought? As I did a bit of research on this, I found the full quote and it reads like this; "the blood of the covenant is thicker than the water of the womb." The bonds we make by choice are of great significance in our lives. We just may not know it at the time.

In the innocent eyes of a young child, my relationship with my childhood best friend meant lots of fun on countless playdates, sleepovers, trips and more. As an adult, this friendship and bond played a significant part in who I am today.

How does one love someone much like a daughter when there is zero DNA? Because she exudes the unconditional love of Jesus. That's how!

My childhood best friend's mom has a beautiful soul. Picture a kind, beautiful, soft-spoken, calm-spirited, loving, devoted Christian woman and you see Lennis. Her motherly love was not only seen and felt by her child but me as well. In her presence, I always felt like I was her second daughter. Beautiful and loved. No strings attached.

With the abundance of baby dolls Shirley and I played with as young girls, I always knew I wanted to be a mom. Could I emulate Lennis as a mother? I hoped one day I would.

I realize all these years later that Shirley's family served as an ideal model of a loving, supportive family. I just didn't know it at the time.

Shirley and I were born and raised in a small rural community. Where everyone knows

"YOU WILL BE ENRICHED IN EVERY WAY TO BE GENEROUS IN EVERY WAY, WHICH THROUGH US WILL PRODUCE THANKSGIVING TO GOD."

2 CORINTHIANS 9:11 ESV

everyone so to speak. One grade separated us in school, but we were members of the same church. That common thread is where our friendship blossomed. One night sleepovers turned to two or three nights with no hesitation from Lennis. I was included in many trips with Shirley and her family. From camping to hotel destinations to Saturday evening trips out to eat at Dairy Treet (our choice of course!). Many included our baby dolls and all their accessories. I'm certain they had their own luggage and with the number of dolls we took with us each trip, it was more than one piece of luggage for our dolls and accessories. Picture two little girls in the backseat of the car and anywhere there was open space, there sat our dolls. They were dressed and ready for the next adventure just like us! I spent countless days and nights with Shirley, and Lennis always nurtured me like her own.

As Shirley and I journeyed our way through elementary school, junior high, high school, graduation, college, marriage, and children, Lennis never wavered. No barriers, no boundaries, no judgment. She was always there for us.

Shirley and I now live in different communities and we're not able to see each other as often as we would like. When we do, we pick up right where we left off. Our families have grown up together and it makes my heart so happy. Shirley's daughter has always called me "Aunt Tyanne" and when our youngest was born, we asked Shirley and her husband to serve as his godparents and they kindly accepted.

My heart longed to be immersed in a calm, tranquil atmosphere. Lennis' home offered me just that. As a child, I was having fun. As an adult, I vowed I would one day equip my family with the same peaceful and loving environment. I have many cherished memories with this loving family that I'm certain would never have happened without God placing them in my life when I needed them the most. I am forever grateful for their unconditional love, heartfelt friendship, and bond throughout these years.

The epitome of unconditional love Lennis portrays in her life as a wife, mother and friend surpass any definition of perfection in my mind. One I strive to achieve daily. I am the woman I am today because of the selfless act of a devoted Christian woman whose name is Lennis. I will always cherish what she has gifted me--the gift of a loving family.

WRITE ABOUT AN INSPIRING WOMAN IN YOUR LIFE

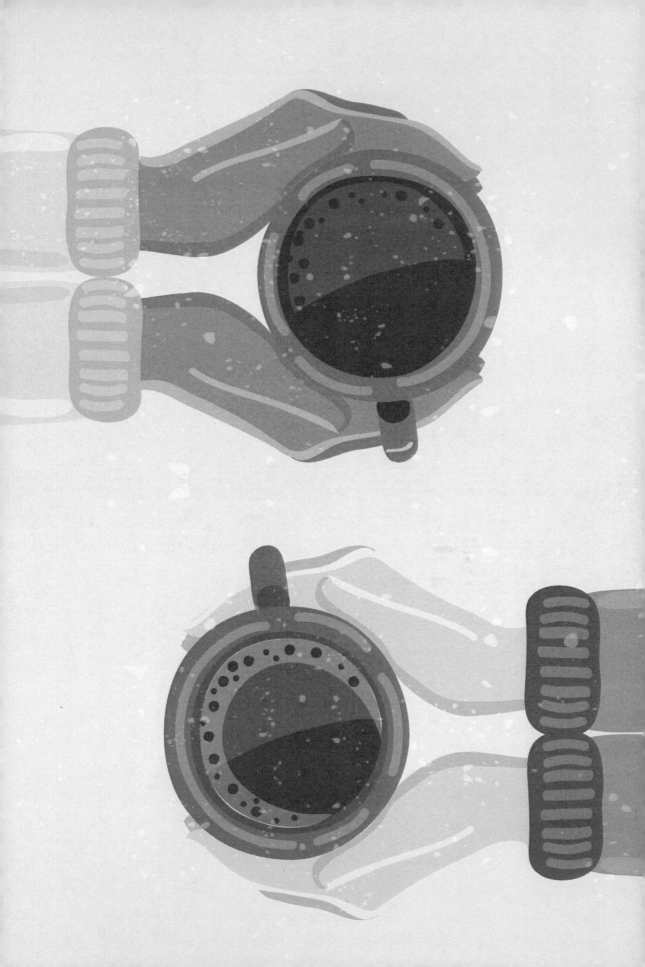

IF ANYONE
HAS THE
world's goods
& SEES HIS
. BROTHER
in Need
YET
CLOSES HIS HEART
AGAINST HIM
HOW
DOES *God's love*
ABIDE
IN HIM ?

1 JOHN 3:17

BEING THE
INSPIRING WOMEN
In Our Circles

Inspiring Women

EXPRESS GRATITUDE

For us to thank God, for anything, we must first realize that all things – EVERY thing – we have is from God.

We can be so selfish, living our lives in a manner where we see everything and everyone revolving around us. Everything is here for me and everything is mine. That sounds harsh, but we are selfish at heart because of our sin nature. It's not something we're taught; we are born with this nature. No? Try taking that toy or blanket or bottle away from a baby! Ha!

As adults, the best weapon we have in our arsenal to fight this vanity is God's Word. And it tells us that in contrast to our "mine" mentality, everything is not ours. Everything, in fact, is God's.

"Every good gift and every perfect gift is from above, coming down from the Father of lights, with whom there is no variation or shadow due to change." James 1:17

"I THANK MY GOD IN ALL MY REMEMBRANCE OF YOU."

PHILIPPIANS 1:3

If we are blessed to have things and people in our lives, these have been given to us my Him also. That job or promotion that we work hard to achieve, it is a gift from God. That house or car or meal or brand name something or other that we just purchased with "my" money, yes, those also are gifts from God.

So, I must ask myself...

If everything I have is indeed not mine but God's, and if everything I have is not something I have earned or deserve, but is a gift from God, why do I not thank Him?

Memories. (que the soundtrack)

I have so many wonderful memories that I love to recall and would go back and visit some of those times or people if I could. But then there's another room in my memory warehouse that I don't like to visit. As beautiful as some memories are, others can be equally not.

In Paul's context (Philippians 1:3) though, he is wanting to encourage the recipients of his letter. He is telling them that he not only remembers them, but that every time he does, he thanks God for them.

How would you feel if that was the opening line of a letter you received? Ok, maybe an email, but all the same, to have someone stop whatever they are doing and take time to tell you that not only are they thinking about you but they are thankful for you. Add the bonus of them thanking God for you because they recognize that you and your relationship are a gift from God?

Make. my. day.

So, I must ask myself...

When was the last time I made someone's day in this manner? No, let's go back farther.

When was the last time I thanked God for the people in my life? And not just the ones who I am happy with or who have done something for me lately.

When was the last time I thanked God for the difficult, disagreeable sandpaper people in my life?

This is soul deep, friends. This is where the seeds are planted. If we truly desire to be women who inspire generations, we must allow God to use His Word to shape our character. I must allow Him to cut straight to the heart of the problem – in my own heart – and plant the seeds of His Word deep – soul deep.

I am definitely being challenged by this, challenged to LIVE IT. How about you?

After all, what value is a "Thank You" if it's never spoken?

Let's be thankful. Offer gratitude. Be Inspiring.

Thankful for You

Has there been a special woman who has inspired your spiritual walk?

I have had several women pour into my life, unfortunately I have not always expressed my gratitude directly to them. In the younger years I probably did not fully realize the impact their love and actions would have on my life. More recently, I missed the opportunity to thank a special woman for her influence in my life and I dearly regret it.

Let's take the time while we are studying about Inspiring Women, to give some recognition and gratitude to the inspiring women who have poured in to our souls.

Use the following blank note pages to write a thank you to each inspiring woman in your life. If any of these women have passed on or you are no longer in contact with them, write the note anyway. Expressing this gratitude is also about giving recognition for what others have done for us and acknowledging God's divine handling of our relationships.

If you are in contact with them, mail them the note. Or better yet, why not contact them directly and arrange a time when you both can get together and continue to pour love into each other's lives.

Feel free to copy these blank note pages to write as many notes as needed.

"ENTER HIS GATES WITH THANKSGIVING, AND HIS COURTS WITH PRAISE."

PSALM 100:4 ESV

FOR BIBLE ART JOURNALERS:

Select a scripture which exemplifies the inspiring character of this special woman. Journal on your page about your gratitude or a specific lesson you learned through your relationship.

The note sheet can also be used as a tip-in to add a longer entry.

Consider adding a favorite photograph as a remembrance of your special relationship. This can also be added as a tip-in. Or make a copy of the photo on clear sticker (label) paper and add directly on the page.

Inspiring Women
GIVE TESTIMONY

Can I share a little truth with you? I have always tensed up a little bit when someone has asked me to share my testimony. And then I feel guilty. I'm a Christian, so sharing one's testimony is standard practice, right?

I mean, talk about an episode of my fav home improvement show, no problem! Send a friend a text about the great deal I just found at the craft store, of course. But sit down with someone and share about the Gospel, paralyzed.

Maybe you feel the same?

"SO THE WOMAN LEFT HER WATER JAR & WENT AWAY INTO TOWN AND SAID TO THE PEOPLE, "COME, SEE A MAN WHO TOLD ME ALL THAT I EVER DID. CAN THIS BE THE CHRIST?."

JOHN 4:28-29 ESV

As I was talking to God about this, He helped me to see that I had a perception problem.

Let's read Psalm 78:1-4 (The Message translation) especially taking note of the tone of the speaker,

> "Listen, dear friends, to God's truth, bend your ears to what
> I tell you. I'm chewing on the morsel of a proverb;
> I'll let you in on the sweet old truths, stories we heard
> from our fathers, counsel we learned at our mother's knee.
> We're not keeping this to ourselves, we're passing it
> along to the next generation— God's fame and fortune,
> the marvelous things he has done."

Did you notice that excitement? That, "I've got something to share and I can't wait to tell you!"?

So why is the Psalmist so excited and I'm so nervous?

The answer is in their words ... "sweet old truths" ... "stories we heard" ... "we're passing it along".

To them, they were simply passing along family stories of how God was present in their lives. Just like when we get together with our families and share the fun and wonderful memories we share with each other. One generation telling the next generation about the past generations.

Ok, I can do this. I can tell others about what God has done in my life, in my family's life and even in the lives of others.

My perception about sharing my "testimony" was all wrong. I thought it had to be some profound Scripture quoting monologue at the end of which the person I was speaking with should fall on their knees confessing their sin. I thought my words should transform someone's life. And that was (IS) a tremendous amount of pressure.

It is also **not true**.

Transforming someone's life is not our job. Read that again. *Transforming someone's life is NOT our job.* It is God's job. God is the transformer. God is the life changer. We are just the story tellers. We are the seed planters.

Is there someone in your circle who needs to hear about what God has done in your life? Pray and ask God to reveal a name. Then ask God to divinely create just the right circumstances so you can share with this person.

Sometimes, the hardest part of sharing about God with someone is starting the conversation.

There are techniques and methods which can be researched on-line, but I have found others most receptive when I share about God in response to their current need.

It may sound simplified, but if your friend was looking for a new couch and you knew of a sale or reputable furniture store, you would pass along that info, right?

God is the answer to our spiritual needs. Maybe your friend is already a Christian. That's ok, share with them about how God met you in your place of need. We are all growing and maturing as Christians and need encouragement from other Christians.

If you find yourself in a conversation and you don't think you have a personal experience with God which translates to their situation, just ask if you can pray for them, right then and there. Take their hands and pray to God together.

On the next two pages is a blog excerpt from BillyGraham.org which shares some tips about sharing your faith. Take some time to think about and write out your personal faith story and then be ready to share when God presents the opportunity.

Sharing your testimony is bold, I know. Ask God for courage, and remember the seeds planted in your life by those inspiring women who gave testimony about what God had done in their lives.

Be bold. Be a seed planter. Be inspiring.

Share True Stories of God's Power

No matter how "ordinary" yours may seem, we've all got a story to tell and you never know what it can mean to someone until you share it. Jesus often talked in parables so people could better grasp God's plans, instructions and power. In the same way, you can use personal experiences and stories to relate to others and tell them about Christ.

Keep in mind, though, that most people will only give you a few minutes to get your point across. So you don't ramble on and on, try writing down your story—focusing on a few key points. Ask God to give you guidance as you write (James 1:5-6). These questions may also help you narrow your testimony down to three minutes or so:

- What was life like before you accepted Christ?

- How did you receive Christ? Why did you choose to put your trust in Him? Try to mention a Bible verse or two, but be careful not to overwhelm your listener.

- How has life changed since accepting Christ? It's OK if you stumbled or struggled in the past. The important thing is to be honest and relatable.

Above all, remember that it's God's business to turn a person's heart towards Christ. Though we are to be obedient in sharing our faith, our persuasion alone is not enough. As 1 Corinthians 3:6 says, some plant, some water, but it is God who makes the seed grow.

Source: BillyGraham.org, "3 Keys to Sharing Your Faith"

Inspiring Women
BESTOW HOSPITALITY

I was gathered with some friends one day and we were sharing with each other about our backgrounds; where we were from, whether or not we went to church growing up, about our family life and so on.

As I recall one friend's story, I'm reminded that something as simple as brownies and popcorn can influence someone's spiritual life. My friend told of not having a stable home life as a young girl and teen, but a friends parents invited her to their house, where brownies and popcorn were always waiting and served with love.

It was a display of Christian hospitality which left a great impression on my friend. She now as an adult gives testimony of all God has done in her life and opens her own home to bestow hospitality to others.

"DO NOT NEGLECT TO SHOW HOSPITALITY TO STRANGERS, FOR THEREBY SOME HAVE ENTERTAINED ANGELS UNAWARES."

HEBREWS 13:2 ESV

Christian hospitality differs from just entertaining.

Entertaining focuses on the host - the home must be spotless, the food must be well prepared and abundant, the host must appear relaxed and good natured.

Hospitality, in contrast, focuses on the guests. Their needs - whether a place to stay, food to eat, someone to listen or acceptance - are the primary concern.

Hospitality can happen in a messy home. It can happen around a dinner table where the main dish is canned soup and sandwiches. It can even happen while the host and the guest are doing chores together.

Yes, hospitality can happen with something as simple as brownies and popcorn.

Hospitality is not about what is served or even where it's served, hospitality is about how it's served - *with a heart overflowing with love*.

When Jesus was questioned about the most important commandment, he responded by quoting an old familiar teaching:

"The most important one," answered Jesus, " is this: 'Hear O Israel: The Lord your God, the Lord is one. Love the Lord your God will all your heart and with all your soul and with all your mind and with all your strength.' (ref: Deuteronomy 6:4-5) *The second is this: 'Love your neighbor as yourself.'* (ref: Leviticus 19:18) *There is no commandment greater than these."* Mark 12:29-31

Is there someone you know who needs to be loved on with hospitality?

Pray and ask God to reveal a name. Then invite them over. Ask them to come sit at your table. Then don't overprepare. Maybe have afternoon coffee or dessert. Maybe have an easy to prepare meal. Focus on your guest. What is their need?

Be a neighbor. Be hospitable. Be inspiring.

Top 4 Hospitality Tips from Mitzi Neely

1. **CELEBRATE.**
   Find joy in the everyday. Take time to laugh and count every blessing. Gratitude and thanksgiving are at the top of the list.

2. **CONNECT.**
   Make time for the people in your life but avoid overextending yourself to the point that you no longer enjoy the fellowship. Plug into your people more than your phone.

3. **CARE.**
   Serve and help out in your community. Make a difference. Invite a friend over for a meal or enjoy a special activity together.

4. **CUT BACK.**
   Minimize the stress, remember less is more. Focus on the people not the busyness. Host a buffet where everyone brings a dish instead of taking responsibility for the entire meal.

Have an Attitude of Hospitality

BE WELCOMING TO EVERYONE YOU MEET. Be kind, even when someone is not kind to you. Their situation may not be known and your expression of under-served kindness my shine the light of Christ they need in their circumstances. Hospitality doesn't just happen in your home, a "friendly reception" can be given to anyone, anywhere.

ENGAGE WITH PEOPLE AND CREATE A PERSONAL CONNECTION. We all gravitate toward people we feel comfortable and find a connection with. Look for the connection with others. Notice the commonalities not the differences. Converse with others with a genuine heart and desire to make them feel comfortable. At the heart of hospitality is "receiving strangers in a friendly way".

GATHER AROUND THE TABLE. Take a que from Christ here, invite others to your table. He often shared meals with others whether he was the host or the guest. Serve your guests, let them know they are important to you and that you desire to meet their needs. Engage with your neighbors and invite them in, especially those whom you do not know well.

PAY ATTENTION TO THOSE AROUND YOU. Notice the unnoticed and the over-looked. God places people in our paths on purpose. Slow down to notice these God appointments then invite the uninvited and discover their need. A great way to do this is to reach out to a visitor at church and invite them to lunch. Treat these "strangers in a generous way".

FOR BIBLE ART JOURNALERS:

Transfer the artwork on the opposite page into your Journaling Bible or journal. Write about a time when someone has shown you hospitality or a divine appoint-ment when God connected you with someone. This color page would also make a great tip-in.

Contribute to the needs of the saints and seek to show hospitality

Romans 12:13

BLANK

INSPIRING WOMEN

Character Study Pages

NAME:

SCRIPTURE:

CHARACTER TRAIT:

OBSERVATION:

INTERPRETATION:

APPLICATION:

MAKE A PLAN:

1. How can we put into practice what we are learning from this passage?

2. Make a plan specific to you: Identify 3 specific actions to take.

3. How can you use what you have learned from (person studied) to build a legacy within your family?

NOTES:

PRAYER:

NOTEWORTHY

NAME:

SCRIPTURE:

CHARACTER TRAIT:

OBSERVATION:

INTERPRETATION:

APPLICATION:

MAKE A PLAN:

1. How can we put into practice what we are learning from this passage?

2. Make a plan specific to you: Identify 3 specific actions to take.

3. How can you use what you have learned from (person studied) to build a legacy within your family?

NOTES:

PRAYER:

NOTEWORTHY

NAME:

SCRIPTURE:

CHARACTER TRAIT:

OBSERVATION:

INTERPRETATION:

APPLICATION:

MAKE A PLAN:

1. How can we put into practice what we are learning from this passage?

2. Make a plan specific to you: Identify 3 specific actions to take.

3. How can you use what you have learned from (person studied) to build a legacy within your family?

NOTES:

PRAYER:

NAME:

SCRIPTURE:

CHARACTER TRAIT:

OBSERVATION:

INTERPRETATION:

APPLICATION:

MAKE A PLAN:

1. How can we put into practice what we are learning from this passage?

2. Make a plan specific to you: Identify 3 specific actions to take.

3. How can you use what you have learned from (person studied) to build a legacy within your family?

NOTES:

PRAYER:

NAME:

SCRIPTURE:

CHARACTER TRAIT:

OBSERVATION:

INTERPRETATION:

APPLICATION:

MAKE A PLAN:

1. How can we put into practice what we are learning from this passage?

2. Make a plan specific to you: Identify 3 specific actions to take.

3. How can you use what you have learned from (person studied) to build a legacy within your family?

NOTES:

PRAYER:

DO YOU KNOW JESUS?

God loves us so much that He sent His Son, Jesus, to die on the cross to pay the price for our sins and bring us into a relationship with Him. (John 3:16) Through Christ, we can know the promise of eternal life and experience the joy of knowing God here on earth!

If you would like to have a relationship with God, the Bible tells us that the first step is acknowledging that we have sinned and that there is nothing we can do to earn God's love (Romans 3:23-26). Next, we believe and confess that Jesus is Lord (Romans 10:9) and allow Him to guide our lives.

Where we once wanted to control our own future, we now invite Jesus into our hearts to be Lord over our lives.

Knowing God's peace, perspective and purpose for your life begins with a personal relationship with Jesus.

Would you like to accept Jesus as Lord of your life? You can pray the following prayer:

Lord, I confess that I have sinned against You and ask You to forgive me. I'm sorry that my sin has hurt You and other people in my life. I acknowledge that I could never earn salvation by my good works, but I come to You and trust in what Jesus did for me on the cross.

I believe that You love me and that Jesus died and rose again so that I can be forgiven and come to know You. I ask You to come into my heart and be Lord of my life. I trust You with everything, and I thank You for loving me so much that I can know You here on earth and spend the rest of eternity with You in heaven.

In Jesus name, Amen

MEET THE AUTHORS

Jana Kennedy Spicer

Founder Sweet To The Soul Ministries, is a wife, mom and Nana. She is a born and raised Texas girl who loves boots, sunflowers and sweet tea. She has a heart for studying God's Word and is passionate about encouraging women to do the same. Her favorite part of ministry is where her faith and art collide! This is the sweet spot where souls become inspired. After a 30 year corporate career, God called her to share her art and love of Bible Study with others. A woman rescued and repaired by the grace of God, she loves to share about the realness of God's love, redemption and faithfulness.

Facebook @Sweet.To.The.Soul.Ministries | Instagram @jana_sweettothesoul
Bible Journaling Facebook & Instagram @SweetToTheSoulShoppe

Mitzi Neely

Mitzi Neely is known for encouraging and inspiring people of all ages through her teachings on grace, love, joy, and peace. Her primary goal is to use her gifts and talents as God leads, always waiting patiently before turning to the right or to the left, listening for His voice saying "This is the way; walk in it." Isaiah 30:21 NIV

Mitzi's heart is to lighten your load, while conveying her message that nobody's perfect. Her desire when she speaks, sings, creates, or instructs is honesty and transparency, such that God receives glory and honor. She is the founder and ministry leader of Peacefully Imperfect and is the author of A Thankful Heart: 30 Days to the Grateful Life, Dwell in the Psalms, and JOY for Everyday Life. Mitzi is also the assistant superintendent of an East Texas school district.

She and her husband, Jerry reside in Longview and enjoy their family and friends when they aren't working on the farm or tending to school.
Follow Mitzi at peacefullyimperfect.net because the joy of the journey is learning His word together.

Stephanie K Adams

Stephanie K Adams is the founding Director of Real Women Ministries, where she equips women with resources for Bible Study and prayer. She is passionate about helping women find time for God's Word in the midst of their busy lives. Stephanie is a Board Certified Advanced Christian Life Coach and author of In the Shadow of the Cross: Following Jesus Through His Last Days and is a contributing author to Bearing Fruit: Living Rooted in Christ.

You can connect with Stephanie at RealWomenMinistries.org

Carmen Horne

Carmen Horne is the author of Out of Words: 31 Prayers of Hope for Your Hurting Heart, Board Certified Advanced Christian Life Coach, and speaker who uses her gifts to encourage women. She is passionate about supporting women through life's challenges as they learn to draw on God's power and a dynamic relationship with Jesus to change their perspective on the unexpected.
Carmen is a beach sitter and dark chocolate nibbler. Her family calls the Bayou State home.

Visit her website's www.carmenhorne.com to learn more about her and her heart for ministry.

Tyanne Rakowitz

I am a woman of God! Uniquely and wonderfully made. Wife to my awesome husband, Bill for 39+ years. Mom to 6; 3 by blood and 3 by love. Grammy to 5 little boys. Planner and organizer extraordinaire!

SWEET TO THE SOUL
FAITH

"*THE INSPIRE JOURNAL*"

SWEET TO THE SOUL'S NEWEST PUBLICATION,

FAITH,

A QUARTERLY JOURNAL ENCOURAGING AND EQUIPPING WOMEN
TO BE THE KINGDOM INFLUENCERS GOD HAS
CALLED US TO BE.

VISIT SWEETTOTHESOULFAITH.COM FOR INFORMATION

COMPANION PRAYER JOURNAL & STUDY

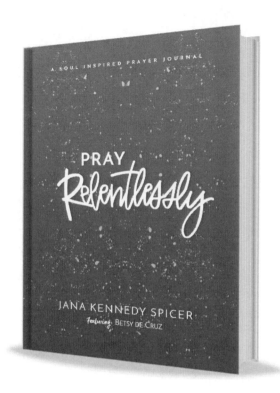

A SOUL INSPIRED PRAYER JOURNAL WITH BIBLE STUDY

Replete with scriptural foundation and thought-provoking questions, *Pray Relentlessly* shores up our faith and motivates us to press forward in our prayer life. To make progress. Steeped in His Truth as we study this prayer journal, we find assurance God deeply desires a personal relationship with us, and that personal relationship requires communication. Prayer. ~ Monica Bard

VISIT SWEETTOTHESOUL.COM/PRAY-RELENTLESSLY FOR INFORMATION

OTHER GREAT RESOURCES

From Sweet To The Soul Ministries

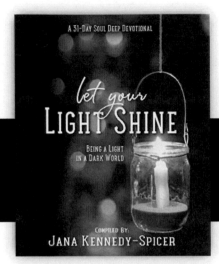

LET YOUR LIGHT SHINE

We live in a dark world, and it seems to be getting darker day by day. Fear, depression, grief, abuse, illness can seem overwhelming. But there is hope. There is a light. *Let Your Light Shine* is a 31-day journey through God's Word to learn about the hope we have in Christ Jesus.

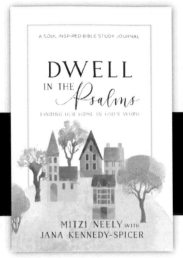

DWELL IN THE PSALMS

In *Dwell in the Psalms*, Mitzi Neely shares beautiful words of encouragement to accept God's invitation to spend time with Him. "My time with God is my dwelling place. The place that prepares me to face my earthly responsibilities."

GRACIOUS WORDS

James warns us that the tongue is small but mighty. The ability to control our tongues and our words comes only through surrendering them to God and allowing the Holy Spirit to intercede. It takes great obedience on our part to keep our words gracious.

JINGLE AND JOY

Jingle and Joy is an advent study, sharing the story of prayer beneath the tree for all people. You will want to keep it by your tree, bedside table, or coffee table to read each day from now until Christmas. Daily prayer prompts will keep you kneeling beneath the tree, looking up to God,

VISIT US ON-LINE

SweetToTheSoul.com

SweetToTheSoulShoppe.com

SOUL INSPIRED SCRIPTURE READING PLANS: Each month consists of a topic-driven reading plan, complete with 31 Scriptures to use in your Bible study and quiet time. The verses serve as a guide to dive deep into God's Word as you focus on small portions. Blank Scripture Journal pages are also available for download.

SOUL INSPIRED BIBLE STUDY RESOURCES: Soul Inspired Bible Study is about spending time in the scripture with God and allowing the Holy Spirit to give us understanding. These Bible Studies cover a variety of topics and offer resources in multiple formats including journals, devotionals and more.

INSPIRED INBOX: These free Soul Inspired Bible Studies are delivered directly to your inbox. Choose from several topics. Just sign up, check your email box, then download and print all your study materials. Study alone at your own pace or invite friends to join you and study the Bible together.

SOUL INSPIRED BIBLE JOURNALING RESOURCES: are designed to inspire your soul and encourage you to use your creativity during your Bible Study time. Our journaling resources include Bible Journaling Kits, printable templates / colorable bookmarks, coloring pages, scripture cards and more!

SOUL INSPIRED COLORING BOOKS: Coloring is a wonderful way to relax and destress. Our coloring books include inspirational Scripture and encouraging quotes through beautifully hand-drawn artwork. Be inspired as you spend time reflecting on scripture as well as enjoying the calming and refreshing benefits of coloring.

SWEET TO THE SOUL SHOPPE: Our on-line shoppe is where you will find all of our Bible Journaling and creative resources. Many resources are printable instant digital downloads. We also have several sets of scripture cards and blank encouragement cards. Visit sweettothesoulshoppe.com to see our full line of products.

Our Bible Studies and Journals are available for purchase via Amazon.
Visit sweettothesoul.com for direct links to each of our books or journals.

SWEET TO THE SOUL
PRESS

SWEETTOTHESOUL.com

Made in United States
North Haven, CT
25 January 2022

15242802R00080